HEALED
Wounds transformed into blessings

ELAINE DASILVA

Preface - Nilce Sousa

HEALED Wounds transformed into blessings
1st edition: 2020
Elaine Dasilva

Edition and Revision: **Suellen de Araújo Costa**
Layout, Cover, Graphic Design: **Marcus V. P. Alcântara**
Editorial Coordination: **Nilce Sousa**
English Edition: **Bianca Alves and Katia Felix**

Published in Brazil by **Cevi Produções**
CNPJ 07.856.521/0001-94
Intagram: @editoracevi
ceviproducoes@gmail.com

D229c Dasilva, Elaine
     Healed : wounds transformed into blessings / Elaine Dasilva; edition and revision: Suellen de Araújo Costa, english edition: Bianca E. Menezes Alves;
editorial coordination: Nilce Sousa. – 1. ed. – Caldas Novas-GO : Cevi Produções,
2020.
     119 p.; 15,24 x 22,86 cm

     Inclui bibliografia
     ISBN: 978-65-5642-022-6.
 1. Healing by faith. 2. Self-help. 3. Miracles. 4. Overcoming. 5. Christian life.

     I. Sousa, Nilce. II. Book title: Curados, feridas transformadas em bênção

                                           CDU: 265.8

Catalogação na publicação por: Onélia Silva Guimarães CRB-14/071

E-mail: contato.elainedasilva@gmail.com
Twitter: @ElaineD27328570
Instagram: @pastoraelaineda
Facebook: Elaine Da Silva
Facebook: Pastora Elaine Da Silva

Biography

Elaine Dasilva is a writer, pastor, speaker, lecturer, and counselor. She works in the field of Psychology, helping the Brazilian, American, and Hispanic families. She is married to Agnaldo Dasilva and has two sons, Andrew and James. They have lived in the Boston area, in the city of Revere, Massachusetts for twenty seven years.

She is the author of two books: Restoration: Leaving the pain behind, and Healed: Wounds transformed into blessings. Her first book was published in three languages, Portuguese, English and Spanish, and the second one in Portuguese and English.

Her purpose is to bring restoration and encouragement to those who have been imprisoned in degrading conditions, in need of physical and emotional recovery, and also to encourage others to be instruments of God in the lives of those who surround them, through instruction and by sharing testimonials of emotional and physical healing.

Dedication

I dedicate this book to my husband Agnaldo, whom I love dearly and who has encouraged me, giving me the support and motivation I needed to continue this journey. You, my dear, are a gift from God in my life.

I also dedicate it to my two sons Andrew and James, who have been a reason of joy in my life. I am grateful to God for their lives, for being such blessings in our family, as well as in the lives of many others surrounding them, for the glory of the Lord Jesus.

Acknowledgments

I thank the Lord Jesus for the care and zeal for my family and I. I am grateful for the healing He has performed in my life, including the healing of past traumas and also for fulfilling yet another of His promises allowing me to write this work to heal, restore and strengthen lives for His kingdom.

I want to thank my husband and children for their effort, support, and dedication. They were the first ones to believe that this work would be done. They also embraced all the challenges a writer faces when working on a book and have been with me every step of the way. I love you.

I would like to thank my parents for praying for me and for the incentive I receive from my siblings, who often leave me encouraging messages incentivizing me to keep writing.

I also thank the Ebenezer Baptist Church for their prayers and support. You are a part of my life. I also extend my gratitude to sister Marlei, for always accompanying me to events and for propagating my books to others with joy.

I thank my friends: Pastor Nilce Souza and sister Katia Felix, and all the team that cooperates so that this evangelistic project can be fulfilled.

Preface

As desired as the healing Path may be, it is not easy. Many people look at it with the wrong lenses, believing that the cure is for others or strangers, especially because we live in a time where we worship what has no meaning and our existence is summarized by the admiration and likes on social networks.

However, nothing can be further from the truth and more superficial than to wait for the cure to take place working on it and towards it. This process starts at home, in the family, the place where all the masks fall and the truth should be faced. True healing, as the author teaches us very well in this book, begins with the person him or herself, and many times the ones closest to them at home, a place where the truth should prevail and be seen clearly

We do not know who we really are until we are confronted, hurt, and then healed. No one is healed if there is no wound. And if there is no wound, we will not see the scars that were caused by our experiences, which led to our learning, and developed the wisdom for a life of achievement and success.

I constantly learn from Elaine, and I call her "my pastor of love." She exhales love in her eyes, her words, and her attitudes. She really has a healed heart and has the authority to teach on the subject. She has learned to renounce her pains and wounds, to dedicate her life for her family and other people that God placed in her path, as many of them had horrible wounds like she had before.

I see in the wounded person two paths: one of eternal wounds, frustrated and bitter living in the shadow of the past mulling over tragedies. And the other, of people who seek God, letting the Holy Spirit bring healing and restoration to their hearts. They left the past behind and moved on towards victory and triumph. There is a saying that I created, and I want to share with you:

"A past badly resolved is never the 'past'; it is always the 'present' ".

I understand that there is no way to be healed by living in the wounds of the past. Pastor Elaine has chosen, decided and persevered on the path of victory and triumph. As I learn from her life, her family and her ministry I know that her heart constantly exhales the anointing power of God's heart which is "love." In this book and in her testimony, you will understand that the greatest weapon she used to be healed was love, which is something natural and truthful in her life.

We were together at the launch of her first book, "Restoration – leaving the pain behind" in New York City. It was incredible to see the difference she made in that environment by showing love to people she had never seen before and many that did not even shared the same faith as her. Her joy and humility was spread to everyone who crossed her path at the event. She does not just teach or preach; she lives a truth in the light of the Gospel and before the Spirit of God.

The miracles that she reports in this material, related to her life, her family and her ministry, are just a sample of the pain she has endured to get here with you in this material. I feel privileged to follow someone so special and important to Jesus.

Read it and learn from her about physical and the most important, the spiritual healing. She doesn't only teach it; she has a healed heart. She chose the best of this life: turning her wounds into blessings, and I suggest to you, who are reading this book, to doing the same; follow the recipe and tips she shares here, her secrets, and the secrets of many people who she has followed in miracles.

Remember that you will not be able to hear God clearly with wounds in your heart, as the bleeding of your emotions may prevent you from hearing His voice within you, and from understanding the prophetic calling He has for you. Be healed and hear the Father speaking to you.

Forgive yourself, seek the Spirit of strength, and follow your life of faith and triumph. The initiation of this process depends on you, more than on God. He will only do, what you allow Him to. Leave behind the stones thrown at you and at your loved ones, cast the past to the past, and have your heart healed. Do as Pastor Elaine did; give up the wounds from childhood and the past, and move on. I love all of you!

Nilce Sousa

SUMMARY

Healed Wounds transformed into blessings

Introduction

Due to the profound childhood traumas that I have suffered, for the longest time, I thought I was born to suffer, to lose my battles, and even to be an insignificant person. My pain was so great that I saw no way out and I thought that if I died, I would be better off. Deep in my shattered emotions, I longed for a different life in which I could overcome all barriers, and be able to move on, but I didn't know how to do it.

My soul was trapped in a sea of sadness and darkness, and my heart was in constant unhappiness and anguish. I was certain that the best thing to do was to end my existence, but, by the mercy of God, before a tragedy happened, He extended His hand, saved and healed me from the intense pain and trauma, and today I can share that deliverance with others.

Before God's transformation in my life, I didn't see much sense in staying alive, and I felt trapped in a tangle of internal problems. Today I find no better way to describe myself but as a white dove flying freely in the bright blue sky.

Today, just like the dove, the bird that symbolizes the Holy Spirit, I can spread my wings hovering free, as I see my reflection in the crystal-clear sea, and bask in the sun as on a beautiful summer day.

Upon receiving the Holy Spirit, our Master, Jesus Christ, officially began His ministry on Earth and commenced to deliver God's message of salvation. Now, I feel free to fly, and go where God wants to take me to bring this message of love and hope to others. I can finally say what the Apostle Paul said:

> *"I have been crucified with Christ and I no longer live, but Christ lives in me. the life I live in the body, I live by faith in the Son of God, who loved me and gave himself for me."*
>
> *Galatians 2:20*

This book that you have in your hands is nothing less than a testimony that this same Jesus can and wants to change your story too. Therefore, I invite you to read it with an open heart, and believe that the process of healing of your pain and suffering can also be a channel of blessings and spiritual enlightenment to others.

Today, years after the Lord has begun this beautiful work in my life, I can tell you that there is no situation in which God cannot act. Even if the barriers that you are facing seem overwhelming, He wants to free you from them and have you moving forward towards your purpose in life.

CHAPTER 1

Complete Restoration

As I share more about myself and what the Lord has done in my life and through my life, I would like to begin by narrating an episode that happened on September 11, 2001, during the terrorist attacks in New York City. That attack was of huge proportion and many lives were claimed then. Everything around the twin towers seemed to have been destroyed, bringing chaos not only to those directly affected but a feeling of commotion and insecurity for the entire world as well. Apparently, there was nothing left.

Our eyes often focus on the superficial; we are in a hurry to draw conclusions and forget to stop and wait for the dust to settle so that we understand that there is more than what meets the eye. To everyone's surprise, "a pear tree called Callery became famous for being a survivor in resisting the terrorist attack on the World Trade Center."

According to the article "National September 11 Memorial & Museum" in October 2001, this tree was discovered with broken roots, burnt branches, and it was severely damaged. Still, it was removed from the rubble by the Park and Recreation Department of New York. After being recovered and rehabilitated, the pear tree was returned to the memorial in 2010.

Everyone knows its past, but the present has become a milestone in US history because it is the symbol of resistance, survival, and new birth. As the Word of God says that a cut down and destroyed tree can be restored, the same way, Jesus can and wants to restore the life of anyone willing to seek His presence.

> *"At least there is hope for a tree: If it is cut down, it will sprout again, and its new shoots will not fail. Its roots may grow old in the ground and its stump die in the soil, yet at the scent of water it will bud and put forth shoots like a plant."*
>
> *Job 14:7-9*

Like a tree that has already been cut down, burned by the fire of adversity, and hat has returned by the smell of the waters of the Lord, so am I. I imagine that you, dear reader, have also experienced hurt and the pain of being emotionally cut by adverse circumstances, but know that He, the Lord, is ready to restore you and make you flourish and fructify again.

No matter how damaged we are, having our roots covered in God's healing waters, make us sprout again. We leave the dryness behind and see our leaves, once dead, reappear green and at the right season, bloom, and generate abundance of life.

This is my main goal in writing this book: to be able to encourage the strengthening of the faith of all those who are having trouble finding hope but have a latent desire to be victorious. As someone that has conquered so many barriers, I can tell you that this is not the time to give up.

Wounds that transform

To me the word wound, has a strong meaning due to the mistreatment, trauma, and frustrations that I have faced, especially during my childhood. We all have a natural tendency to avoid being hurt because we fear our emotional, spiritual, and physical death. Pain and suffering are inevitable. However, these stages of the journey teach us new lessons and enable us with the strength for what is yet to come. An aggravating factor in this process is that many people don't break this vicious cycle and keep hurting others as a result of their own wounds.

In an attempt to hide their pain, some people close their hearts, isolating themselves, and will not recover. Others still blame themselves for what happened and, besides not forgiving themselves they hold grudges and resentment against the real aggressors.

We can't always understand why we go through pain, suffering, wounds, and anguish. I confess that I did not understand the reason for having to experience such distressing moments by having Fibromyalgia. All the sleepless nights, the lack of strength to move around, the shortage of response from health care workers, and the constant criticism of those who had no idea of my suffering, and what I was going through.

Today, even though I am still waiting for my physical healing, I know that God has allowed all this pain to happen in my life in order for Him to create the necessary space to work in me and through me; changing my character, building my confidence and self-esteem, leading me to understand that He has already enabled me for the great work He wants me to do and making clear that He is in control of my life.

It was through this process of pain that I was able to gain more experiences and intimacy with God. My prayer life intensified, and I have learned to persevere when my prayers are not answered in the way I wanted or at the time I wished for. My faith grew, and I became more resilient when fighting the spiritual world and when working in the area of deliverance and spiritual healing. The Bible became my daily manual.

I surrendered myself entirely to God, who now uses me as an instrument of healing to many people in different cities, states, and countries. I have learned that I am strong in Christ Jesus. I have also learned to be more grateful for everything in all areas of my life. Whether things are good or I am facing difficult days, whether in pain or health, whether facing abundance or having very little, I am grateful and content.

I don't live trapped in my past, nor in the after-math reflected in my body. Today I have a new identity in Jesus, my heavenly Father. I've learned to love God above all else, and with that, I have also learned to forgive and love people regardless of the circumstances.

My love for God is not based on what He gives me, but on what He is in my life, and with faith, I look forward to the promise to live what "No eyes have seen, nor ears have heard" (see 1 Corinthians 2:9), and moreover I know that nothing can separate me from the love of Jesus:

> *"For I am convinced that neither death nor life, neither angels nor demons, neither the present nor the future, nor any powers, neither height nor depth, nor anything else in all creation, will be able to separate us from the love of God that is in Christ Jesus our Lord."*
>
> *Romans 8:38-39*

I feel privileged by God for being chosen to preach His word and have the opportunity to share my testimony with you, my dear reader. Healed from many traumas, I can confidently declare that despite the difficulties of the journey, I rejoice in God for the victories He has given me so far, and for being an instrument of restoration in the lives of so many, which I wish to continue doing until the return of Jesus. God turned my tears into joy and wants to do the same for you.

This same hope and transformation are available to everyone who reads this book. Our God is the same, and He is willing to walk with you and give you the healing you need. Remember that your wounds will be healed if you continue to believe and seek the face of God, for you are more than a conqueror in Christ Jesus.

CHAPTER 3

Healed to heal

As part of my ministry, God has provided me with the opportunity to bring the Gospel of salvation to many people in different places. I have been privileged to see countless people surrendering their lives to Christ, and being healed from physical, emotional and spiritual illnesses. I thank God for changing my life and making me a participant in the transformation of others.

I confess that I spent hours meditating on the greatness of God, thanking Him for His love for my life and all humanity, thinking of this inexplicable favor towards us and how He loves us with His agape love. Agape is a word of Greek origin used in the Bible to describe God's love for us as it speaks of something perfect, unparalleled, and immeasurable. Let's see what the Word of God says about this love:

> *"This is how God showed his love among us; He sent his one and only son into the world that we might live through him. This is love: not that we loved God, but that he loved us and sent his son as an atoning sacrifice for our sins."*
>
> *1 John 4: 9-10*

The greatness of God's love cannot be described in words. He takes in His hands a defeated, broken, and empty life, as was mine, and works miracles that no man would be able to perform. He works His miracles in the spiritual realm and allows us to achieve what He has promised us in the physical world.

The promise

I remember this pastor, a man of integrity and truth, who, directed by God, told me that God had great purposes for my life. He also reminded me that the healing I would experience would be used to heal others who needed to be reached by the same grace. My testimony would serve to help people that are emotionally shattered and damaged from traumas they have faced in their path to overcome their own circumstances.

He also told me that I was being prepared for the ministry of deliverance to be an instrument used by God, as He wants to free lives by the power of His name. For God there is nothing impossible. Impossibility is something that resides only in men.

Therefore, beloved reader, do not give up on your desire to receive your victory, whatever your problem is, receive the victory in Jesus' name. Stop reading for a few minutes and say a prayer, surrendering everything before God, giving Him the liberty to work in your life.

Remember that for God, every problem has a solution. According to His will and the time He has determined, He will give you the answer you need. God knows what is best for you. Just believe in Him and surrender it all to His care. See what the Lord Jesus said:

> *"With man this is impossible, but with God all things are possible."*

> *Mathew 19:26*

God's promises did go beyond that Pastor's message. In my pre-teen years, I felt the presence of God and heard His voice in different ways: through His Word, through dreams and revelations, and as a soft voice in my ear or my heart. As time passed, my willingness to be used to transform lives and do God's work, became stronger.

The problems and difficulties I faced at home were no match for my intimacy with God. I could feel that loving friendship involving me daily, and giving me the grace I needed to continue. I am so happy to know that the Word of God remains forever and that when He speaks, what He says will come to fruition:

> *"God is not a man, that he should lie, nor a son of a man, that he should change his mind. Does he speak and then not act? Does he promise and not fulfill?"*

> *Numbers 23:19*

Wounds transformed into beauty

My journey of faith has not been an easy one. However, the battles, victories, and redirection of God have given me the privilege to witness extraordinary miracles, not only in my life, my husband Pastor Agnaldo's life, the lives of our two children, but also in the lives of my family members, friends, members of the Ebenezer Baptist Church, and even in the lives of several other people from the places/cities I have been at.

Over thirty years ago, I heard that my battles would serve for the improvement of others. I confess that it did not sound very attractive to me. The correlation between suffering and being available to bless others may even seemed crazy. However, despite the fact that I was still a child, my desire was directed to bless others and be a friendly shoulder to those who felt abandoned and with no sense of belonging.

Over the years, God turned my tears into laughter, wounds into beauty, sadness into joy. Through this process, I have contemplated His greatness. My healing journey led me to live experiences that were made possible due to my cure's process.

It was not my kindness that brought me here, but the powerful hand of God and His plans to make us spiritually prosperous and able to share with others the miracles done by Him. The feeling of being hurt, lonely and without protection is not strange to me. Having to find the strength to pick up the pieces in which we were broken and to put together the puzzle of a new life healed from traumas, can only completely happen when we let God visit us and fill up the gaps in our being.

In this book, you will read testimonies of what God has accomplished through my life, and also in the lives of people, we love very much, people that have allowed us to minister in their churches, at conferences, through lectures, seminars, vigils, home visits, mission trips and many other places where GOD has directed us to go. I invite you to be receptive to what He wants to do in your life for the Glory of His name.

CHAPTER 4

Involved in His glory

"My soul thirsts for God, for the living God. When can I go and meet with God?"

Psalm 42:2

Summer mornings create such an inviting environment for a stroll around the neighborhood, to go shopping, and opening the house for fresh air. Still, on July 29, 2019, I was in my moment of prayer, alone with God in my room, and I felt such a need to stay there in His presence and be totally involved in His glory. No outside force would be able to take away my desire to be there or dissipate my thirst for His presence.

The presence of God was so intense that I didn't notice the hours passing. That was one of many moments of intimacy and spiritual renewal in God's presence and a time I can hear his voice so deeply that it significantly impacted me.

In prayer moments like this one, God by His mercy, and knowing the needs of His servants, reveals to me even what people are thinking, especially if there is an evil strategy to destroy someone's life through suicide, the breakup of marriages and other serious problems. God reveals Himself to those who seek His face with sincerity and fear.

> *"The Lord confides in those who fear him; he makes his covenant known to them."*
>
> *Psalm 25:14*

While I was praying for people who were supporting me with my first book "Restoration – Leaving the Pain Behind" and dedicating the book to the Lord, God brought to my memory the promise that I was healed so that through my life, others could be healed as well.

That is something that everyone who wants to be healed needs to know: God does not act in our lives so we will cross our arms and stay still. We have the responsibility of sharing God's work in us and allow the Holy Spirit to do his part.

In that moment, amid tears of joy and satisfaction, God gave me the title of this new book. With that, came the confirmation that this book will reach the hands of many people who are looking for a cure and of those who help others to be healed and also in the hands of people who don't even know how much they need God's healing.

So, I quickly wrote the title on a piece of paper and happily celebrated God's direction once again. Five months later, on December 28, 2019, I felt compelled by God to start writing this new work, Healed — Wounds transformed into blessings.

Each testimony, each story shared is for the growth of your faith and renewal of your hope. As you identify with the stories mentioned here, declare victory for your life. Make the decision to be healed and to let God into the most painful areas of your being. Begin to declare God's deliverance over you. For all you need is to believe, and you will see the Glory of God.

The power of the Resurrection

"Did I not tell you that if you believed,
you would see the glory of God?"

John 11:40

Do you remember Martha when her brother Lazarus had been dead for four days? These were Jesus' words to her, as you will read countless times in this book: for God, nothing is impossible, and even if someone is dead, they will live.

Martha and her sister Mary were desperately crying; they thought that after the death of their brother Lazarus, Jesus couldn't do anything more for him and for them. In our limited minds, death is the end of everything, and the pain of losing a loved one is something we cannot explain.

I believe that you, like me, have already lost people that were close and important to you, and depended entirely on Jesus' strength to restore and heal your heart wounded by your loss. Jesus loved Lazarus' family and was interested in everyone's wellbeing; the biblical passage mentions that Jesus even wept.

To the general surprise, Jesus asked for the stone to be removed, and then he ordered: "Lazarus, come out!" At that very moment, Lazarus heard His voice and obeyed His command. He had been dead for four days; he smelled terrible, but death had no power over Lazarus' life, and the power of God was manifested at that moment.

I can say with certainty that just as Jesus raised Lazarus from the dead, I prophesize that in His name, the dreams you, perhaps, gave up on, will also rise for the glory of God. The stone that prevents you from receiving your victory will be removed entirely from your life in the name of Jesus.

From our perspective, the fact that Lazarus and his family were friends with Jesus, and having to go through all that pain, doesn't seem to make much sense. We may think that God's friends should have been immune from suffering. However, when we see his resurrection, we understand that the name of God needed to be glorified.

The same happens to us: how many unexpected things happen in our lives, at times that seem so inconvenient, like the loss of a loved one, a trauma that destroys your joy and dreams, a disappointment with a friend you considered close, frustrations with family members, spouse's infidelity, diagnosed with a severe illness, or any other situation that destabilizes us.

Every single one of these situations imposes a potential devastation and destruction of joy and motivation. However, none of them can make us forget that Jesus is in control, even when everything seems lost.

God uses things that are practically destroyed and works great miracles through that situation. Remember what our Master taught us:

> *"Are not two sparrows sold for a penny? Yet not one of them will fall to the ground apart from the will of your Father. And even the very hairs of your head are all numbered."*
>
> *Mathew 10:29-30*

That shows us that even if we do not understand the reason for specific circumstance, what is important is to know that God has the best for each one of us and never loses control of any situation.

 ELAINE DASILVA

Healed Wounds transformed into blessings

CHAPTER 5

Perseverance in weakness

"But God chose the foolish things of the world to shame the wise; God chose the weak things of the world to shame the strong. He chose the lowly things of this world and the despised things — and the things that are not — to nullify the things that are, so that no one may boast before him."

1 Corinthians 1:27-29

I would like to share with you that despite being healed of my childhood traumas, I still deal with some of the damaging physical and emotional consequences from the suffering I experienced at that time. I have been diagnosed with a condition called Fibromyalgia for over a decade. The news of this diagnosis temporarily stole my freedom, my dreams and my desire to live (I hope with the grace of God, to write a book on this subject in the coming years). Try to mentally picture someone in your life who is active, lively, cheerful, organized, creative with her home decoration, whimsical to the extreme. Someone with an impeccable home, with polished furniture and shiny floors, kitchen cabinets neatly organized and smelling fresh. Someone who reflects this same notion, dedication and love for the work of God in church. Well, this would have been the best description of me until the beginning of my second pregnancy.

In addition to the typical symptoms of feeling sick and tired, as most of the pregnancies tend to have, I realized that my body was experiencing a different type of pain. The impression I had was that all my bones seemed to be broken, taking a breath caused me to ache, and none of my body's movements would go unnoticed.

In addition to the physical symptoms, those pains and discomfort started to invade my soul. I began to experience deep sadness more often than not. Little did I know that the sorrow and anguish I was experiencing were also effects of the medical condition in which I found myself in.

Desperate thoughts invaded my mind, telling me that I could no longer be the same person I was before. My entire life changed overnight, and the possibility of being confined to a wheelchair became part of my reality. I would walk very slowly holding to the walls in order to go from one room to the next in my home, the very home I was able to take such good care of before.

Time passed, and there was no sign of improvement. Amid this chaos, my youngest son was born, and I found myself in a frantic situation. The pain that used to be stronger in the lower back had now spread to the legs and the rest of my body. My husband, Pastor Agnaldo, grieved from seeing me suffering and would verbalize his desire to be able to switch places with me and take my suffering away.

Those were challenging times that often led to despair, and to top it off, there was the pain caused by the criticism of those who did not understand the situation, which made the burden even more difficult to bear. Amid that gale of pain and lack of support, God in His infinite grace led me to pray incessantly for my healing.

I prayed day and night, weeping and crying, and because the movement of my lips caused pain, I continued my cry for help in my mind. I knew that only Jesus Christ could heal me, and I was not willing to give up.

Most people with generalized Fibromyalgia like mine are bound to have limited mobility which restricts the amount of activities they can perform as well. Simple tasks like washing and drying your hair will become a science project. Despite all of that, I wasn't willing to be stopped by anything. I decided that regardless of the pain, I would rise to the occasion and I would bless others and carry forward the message of the cross.

I am aware that the strength I felt and feel does not come from me, because I am still limited. With that being said, I decided to surrender myself entirely to God, developing a deeper relationship with HIM, and as the days passed, I had the conviction that God was not surprised by my situation and that, even though my complete healing was not manifested, as much as I longed for it, nothing was out of His control: See what Psalm 139 says:

     ELAINE DASILVA

> *"For you created my inmost being;
> you knit me together in my mother's womb.
> I praise you because I am fearfully and
> wonderfully made; your works are wonderful,
> I know that full well. My frame was not
> hidden from you when I was made in the
> secret place. When I was woven together in
> the depths of the Earth, your eyes saw my
> unformed body. All the days ordained for me
> were written in your book before one of them
> came to be."*

> *Psalm 139:13-16*

I cannot give you an explanation of why I have not been cured from Fibromyalgia yet. Still, I know that I have exceeded all expectations in terms of leading a healthy and active life, as I am able to perform many activities other patients with this extreme condition have not been able to overcome. I believe that in God's time like it was with my emotional healing, He will heal me. But regardless of this healing, I want to dedicate myself to the work of Christ and be able to speak like the apostle Paul sais at the end of his life: "I have fought the good fight, I have finished the race, I have kept the faith." (2 Timothy 4:7).

Surrender of the Free Will

I don't want my will to be done, but the will of God. I want to live in His presence every day of my life. Many men and women in the Bible faced situations that we do not know if we would be able to face them today. Let's look at Job's case: he was a man of integrity who served God with fear and dedication, and it was so evident, that even the devil noticed Job's faithfulness.

Despite Job not being guilty of anything, God allowed him to lose all he had, including his children, his wealth, his comforts, and his health. Job was judged by those who claimed to be his friends. His wife suggested he should deny God and die. However, God had not lost control of that situation, and Job's destiny would not be marked by the defeat that many expected.

God stood up in favor of His servant and restored his health, his wealth, and returned his joy. Even though he was a righteous man before this great battle, Job now said to God: "My ears had heard of you but now my eyes have seen you." (see Job 42:5). Due to his experience with God, Job could now understand that God was greater than he could have imagined.

That has been how God shows his power in my life. Each morning I experience more of God's supernatural power. I have learned to depend on Him and cast all my anxiety before Him because He cares for my life, as the Apostle Peter teaches us: "Cast all your anxiety on Him because He cares for you." (1 Peter 5:7).

Testimonies like Job's and also this new spiritual level that I am experiencing, encourage me and gives me the confidence that the best of what the Lord has for my life is yet to come. I know that He is the Jehovah-Rapha, the God who heals, and at the right time, as He sees fit, I am sure that He will grant me victory in my health as well.

Let me emphasize that this situation with my health does not obstruct my mind and heart from being very grateful to God for what He has done to me since my childhood. The impact that His presence has on me has changed how I react to daily circumstances today. The subject of suffering, reminds me of the apostle Paul, when he prayed to God asking Him to remove the thorn from his flesh:

> *"To keep me from becoming conceited because of these surpassingly great revelations, there was given me a thorn in my flesh, a messenger of Satan, to torment me. Three times I pleaded with the Lord to take it away from me. But he said to me, 'My grace is sufficient for you, for my power is made perfect in weakness. Therefore, I will boast all the more gladly about my weaknesses, so the Christ's power may rest on me. That is why, for Christ's sake, I delight in weaknesses, in insults, in hardships, in persecutions, in difficulties. For when I am weak, then I am strong."*

> *2 Corinthians 12:7-10*

God's answer was clear and direct to the Apostle Paul, and it has been to me as well. God's power is perfected in our weakness. We do not know and do not even want to speculate what was the thorn in Paul's flesh. What we know and what interests us is that the grace of God was sufficient to him, and such was the anointing over Paul's life and ministry that his aprons were used to heal people. Look:

> *"God did extraordinary miracles through Paul, so that even handkerchiefs and aprons that had touched him were taken to the sick, and their illnesses were cured and the evil spirits left them."*

> *Acts 19:11-12*

CHAPTER 6

Marked by the supernatural

"You were chosen by God to change the lives of many people. God has given you the gift of healing and He will use you in the same way that He uses your mother."

Coronel Fabriciano, 1984.

These words echo in my mind since that night when I was a pre-teen. I can't forget that friendly and humbled Pastor that was willing to deliver God's loving message to me. My mother has been an example of prayer and seeking the Lord's presence. She was always ready to pray for everyone who needed prayers. My brothers and I were eyewitnesses so many times of several miracles and wonders worked by God's hands through her life.

I confess that when the pastor told me about God's plans of using me in the healing ministry, I had spiritual battles in my mind, that wanted to convince me I should not lay my hands on sick people around me. I questioned myself constantly. What would happen if they were not healed? How would I explain what God did not do? How can healing happen through a person like me? Who am I? How can a person who has been emotionally abused have the authority of God to pray for others?

All these questions played over and over in my mind, and I fought them vigorously because even though I still did not have a deep intimacy with God at that time, I did not let go of the desire to obey Him and fulfill his plans for my life.

Independently of my feeling of lack of capacity and being scared of what I could face, I started to do what God called me to do. I began by to praying for people, not only for health-related needs and God started to answer their requests and heal them from illnesses as well. That way, God strengthened my ministry while surprising me constantly.

Healing of the child

There was an occasion, while my husband was preaching in our congregation, and I was praying for him and the church, as I usually do. I then began walking around the church, going row by row until I got to in constant prayer.

Everything seemed quite normal until my eyes caught the tired look of a mother holding her two-year-old daughter. When I inquired about the child's well-being, the mother casually informed me that she had the flu. I laid my hands on the child and rebuked the flu and fever in Jesus' name.

On a following service, I was pleasantly surprised when that mother testified in the congregation that for the glory of God and also for my joy, the child had been completely healed. But the blessing did not stop there, the child had also been cured of a lactose intolerance she had since birth.

The consequences of this condition are painful and can even cause generalized inflammation of several organs. However, after the prayer the child could now drink her yogurt, enjoy puddings and other milk products without any symptoms or side-effects. Hallelujah!

That is how I have seen God's healing and miracles happening. He goes beyond what I ask him for while I am praying for people and visits their health in a complete and miraculous way. God continuously amazes me with the way He answers my prayers. In this instance with the little girl, the prayer was made for the flu, but God knew that the child's life needed an even greater miracle. He healed her beyond what was asked. I glorify God, Jehovah-Rapha, the God who heals.

"He heals the brokenhearted and binds up their wounds."

Psalm 147:3

Healed women

I am convinced that God has called me to preach the Gospel and to show His love and power to all people. Something particularly special to me is the opportunity to speak to and for women. That warms my heart and fills me with happiness.

In 2019 I was invited to speak at a woman's retreat here in the US. That was a 3 day event. We felt the power of God and the operation of the Holy Spirit tangibly. God worked many healings and miracles during those days and on the second night one testimony in particular touched me deeply:

A woman approached the altar and asked us to pray for her because she was ill. She told us that the doctors had already exhausted their options and prescribed everything they could to make her feel better, but there was no improvement in her condition. As there was a lot of noise around us while she reported her problem, I understood that her problem was in her spine, and I prayed with faith for her healing.

The next morning, she testified about the healing she had received from her back pain. She stated that when she got back to her room, she could jump on the bed and move her spine from side to side, and experienced no pain. She was totally healed. After testifying about her cure, she also informed me that I had not understood her prayer request the night before. Her actual condition extreme headache accompanied of a feeling of heaviness and congestion in her nostrils and I had prayed for her back pain instead.

I then prayed for her a second time, and God completed His work in her life. At the time of that prayer she vomited some substance that was inside of her, and from that moment on, she felt completely better and healed for the glory of Jesus Christ. God had a higher purpose in her life. It is He who acts, and His action goes beyond what we understand, everything happens His way and at His determined time.

"For from him and through him and to him are all things. To him, be the glory forever! Amen."

Romans 11:36

There are times when people tell me their needs when asking for prayers, and other times God reveals their needs to me in a surprising way. I remember an episode that happened at one of our local women's group meetings. One of the attendees invited her friend to join us for the first time. Everything went beautifully and smoothly. As a started to pray for the attendees God made me feel that I needed to pray for this specific visitor more intensely.

Until that moment, I had no idea of the dilemma in her life. She had been diagnosed with cancer. In addition to the scary and dangerous diagnosis, she could not count on her husband for support as he was an unwise man who mistreated her for being ill. Also, she was suffering from depression, anxiety, panic attacks, and other problems.

Even without knowing any details of her diagnosis I laid my hands on her to pray, and God revealed her health condition to me. As I continued to pray, I could see when a giant ball of fire descended on her head and completed involved her, and miraculously she was instantly healed. The impact was so significant that all the other women attending that event cried of happiness and glorified God.

Like any prudent person, she went back to her doctors, and once the tests were done, they could not find any of the lymphomas. With that, even the field of medicine testifies that she is healed. How great was our joy when she testified her miracle in person in the presence of everyone in the church. Everyone rejoiced with the power of God, and His holy name was once again glorified. Today, that young lady lives a healthy life; she is happy, serves God, has a job, and also has been healed of her emotional wounds. Hallelujah! God is good.

CHAPTER 7

God's power in action

During these 15 years since my diagnosis, I have experienced the glory of God in my life and witnessed His power in action. Amongst the many testimonies I can remember, I want to share with you another one that is vivid in my mind.

At the time of the event, my husband and I were hosts of a radio program on 1300 AM, a Radio Station in the Boston area, and a listener called us with a prayer request. My husband and I divided the tasks and responsibilities, and while he was live sharing the word of God, I answered prayer requests over the phone in another room.

While praying for a specific person, God revealed me some details about her life and urged me to tell her how much God loved her and that He was taking care of her. It was a moment of communion and real presence of God. I could hear the happiness in her voice. After the prayer, she asked me for the address of the church and said that she would come to meet us in person.

She eventually came to our church and started visiting us more frequently. God still had more to do in her life and at one of my subsequently prayer times, God revealed me something more about her health and ordered me to call her. She was a very private person, and what I would share with her, could only have come from heaven.

She was caught by surprise when I said: "God says that today He delivers you from the grave, and that you are cured from the cancer that afflicts you. The doctors have said that there isn't anything else that can be done and your heart has accepted this result, but God changes your history today!"

Even through the phone, I could feel a strong power coming from heaven; I felt like the floor of my office was shaking under my feet; it felt like I was with her in person. She began to cry because, as I mentioned, she was a private person and had not shared her condition with anyone. The tumor was already a stage four cancer. There were no longer any human resources to help her.

For my spiritual enlightenment, she shared that she had come home from the hospital a few minutes before my call to her. During this visit, the doctor updated her on the results of the new tests and the biopsy that had been done a few days earlier. He informed her that she only had a few days to live. We cried together and thanked God for the miracle and deliverance as she had returned from the hospital, accepting the death sentence set by the results presented by the doctor.

As connoisseurs of the Holy Bible, we can testify that man does not have the last word. Independently of whoever he or she is and whatever position they may occupy, our lives are subjected to the lordship of Christ, and He is the only one who can determine the end of existence.

God had decided that she would live longer, and the tests that were retaken after the prayer confirmed the miracle. She returned to the hospital for new tests and the same doctor who had delivered the news that she was dying, had the privilege of informing her that the cancer that had previously spread throughout her body was now gone. She was fully healed for the Glory of God. Jehovah-Rapha, the God who heals, healed her.

"Surely he took up our infirmities and carried our sorrows, yet we considered him stricken by God, smitten by him, and afflicted. But he was pierced for our transgressions, he was crushed for our iniquities, the punishment that brought us peace was upon him, and by his wounds we are healed."

Isaiah 53:4-5

You and your home

"They replied: Believe in the Lord Jesus, and you will be saved, you and your household."

Acts 16:31

On another occasion, in 2016, after preaching at a woman's congress here, in the United States, the Pastor of the church asked me to anoint the hands of the people who were going to worship God with their offerings and to pray for all of them as well.

I recall that a long line formed in front of me and that about halfway through the line, there was a lady who when I touched her hands manifested a reaction of pain. Her hands looked swollen to the point that they seemed to glow, I could tell that something was not quite normal.

When asked about that condition, she shared that she had rheumatism in her entire body, and added that for some time, she had been unable to wear her wedding ring due to swelling and pain. Her feet also had the same symptoms, and she had arrived there in a wheelchair, with the help of a friend.

The Holy Spirit moved me at that very moment and God used me to prophesy the immediate cure of that condition. And, to the glory of His name, at the end of the event, she showed me that her hands and feet were already returning to normal and that the swelling was disappearing.

As God always confirms His work, imagine my joy when meeting her again at a baby shower of a young woman who attends our church. I could see a beautiful, smiley, and happy woman who came to me identifying herself as the person who had been healed at that congress. She helped me to remember who she was and shared that when she got home after that meeting, she was completely healed.

That was a great encounter. Her happiness was such that she jumped, danced, paraded in front of me, and said that now she could even wear "pointy shoes", which would never be possible before due to the pain she used to feel. She showed me with satisfaction that in addition to her wedding ring, she could also wear the rings that she had been unable to wear for such a long time. Weeks later, she gave us the privilege to come to one of our women's group events and testified what God had done, to honor His name.

Time passed, and on an unexpected day, this same woman came to visit us during our intercession service. I was happy to see her, especially since it was not my usual day to be attending the church meeting. But this time, her face showed concern.

As I approached her, she told me that she was not there for herself, but for her mother-in-law, who was terminally ill with AIDS. That devastating disease caused her body to be covered with wounds and she was clearly living her last days.

Her husband, who had contracted the disease during a blood transfusion at the hospital transmitted the virus to her before he was diagnosed and had recently passed away. The family was emotionally devastated by the possibility of losing her as well.

Her daughter-in-law, who had experienced a miracle and knew that God is the same, and could work in her mother-in-law's life and change her luck, was there asking for prayer. With strong faith she made her prayer request, trusting that even though she could not stay for the meeting she knew God would operate the miracle in her mother-in-law's life.

I immediately summoned some of the meeting attendees and a deacon who was there to pray with me, and as we prayed, I could feel the pain the mother-in-law was feeling. God has given me this sensitivity when I am praying for severe situations.

We prayed for longer than we expected and stayed there in the presence of God, and He was directing us on how to pray and intercede for that situation. We prayed for her

     ELAINE DASILVA

and her family only that night. No matter how many times I attempted to pray for other issues and people, the Holy Spirit led me to pray for her again until the end of that meeting. God had determined her healing that night.

> *"In the same way, the Spirit helps us in our weakness. We do not know what we ought to pray for, but the Spirit himself intercedes for us with groans that words cannot express."*
>
> *Romans 8:26*

We ended our prayer time and returned to our homes, hopeful of God's miracle. After a few days the daughter-in-law called to say that her mother-in-law no longer had any wounds on her body. New medical tests had been done and doctors found that she no longer had HIV, the virus that causes AIDS. Hallelujah. I never had the opportunity to meet the mother-in-law in person, but the story of her miracle impacted my life. The Bible tells us:

> *"Heal the sick, raise the dead, cleanse those who have leprosy, drive out demons. Freely you have received, freely give."*
>
> *Mathew 10:8*

> *"I tell you the truth, anyone who has faith in me will do what I have been doing. He will do even greater things than these, because I am going to the Father."*
>
> *John 14:12*

Jesus invites us to exercise our faith and not forget that we have been healed to be used to heal others. Put on your courage and start looking for the face of God for yourself and everyone around you, and you will see what God is capable of doing.

CHAPTER 8

Learning from pain

There were many experiences in which I could see God using me to manifest His healing to others. I would like to dedicate this chapter to share what God has taught me personally on this subject.

> *"And we know that in all things God works for the good of those who love him, who have been called according to his purpose."*
>
> Romans 8:28

Gratitude

In seeking my cure after the Fibromyalgia diagnosis, my intimacy with God, and my search for His presence intensified. At first, my pursuit was almost singularly for my physical healing, but as time went by, my focus became on getting to know God closer, to seek His face. So, I spent hours talking to God, and I realized that the miracles worked by Him through my life multiplied, and His hand worked in a supernatural way, even more, each day.

In this process, I learned to be happy with God even in times of intense pain. Daily bible readings strengthened me and taught me to praise God regardless of the circumstances around me. We need to seek His presence for He is our joy. Let's reflect a little on the words of the Apostle Paul:

> *"I am not saying this because I am in need, for I have learned to be content whatever the circumstances. I know what it is to be in need, and I know what it is to have plenty. I have learned the secret of being content in any and every situation, whether well fed or hungry, whether living in plenty or in want. I can do everything through him who gives me strength."*
>
> *Philippians 4:11-13*

My gratitude to God goes beyond the joy that He brings me during the days of pain, anguish, and despair. It includes the opportunity to witness Him healing people of incurable diseases through my life. No matter how painful your journey may be, make being grateful a part of your daily spiritual exercise, as we always have reasons to be appreciative.

Testify your miracles

Another thing that God has shown me insistently and you may see it repeatedly on the pages of this book is that

He heals us in order to use us to heal others. This truth goes beyond the duty of gratitude. It is very fulfilling when we stop orbiting around our pains and can offer some solace to those in need of help.

That's why I ask you not to be silent about what God has done in your life. Open your mouth and testify, sharing His work so that others can be edified. Your testimony can be an incentive for others to continue their search for God.

I have no words to express the joy I feel when I hear people declaring that if I, Pastor Elaine, who have been through so many situations and experiences have won my battle, so will they. That is one more indication that our pain, experiences, and history of restoration can edify those who have heard our testimonies.

Sanctification

One key that God has given me is the consecration or sanctification. This is a process of total and absolute surrender of our own will in order for Him to work in us and through us. The life of a genuine Christian goes through the steps of: "deny himself" (see Luke 9:23) and a continued search for His presence, whether the circumstances are favorable or not.

As a pastor, I never approach the pulpit of our local church or churches where I am preaching at, without preparing myself with many hours of prayer, study of the word, and seeking the presence of God. Doing God's work is not like going to a casual meeting with friends. We need to be prepared and understand that we are fighting an invisible battle that does not stop.

Our God enables us and strengthens us to win; however, we need to do our part in the process of sanctification. That is our responsibility before God. Every sacrifice we make to have more of God's presence is valuable, and He rewards us for that.

Zeal

> *"For zeal for your house consumes me,*
> *and the insults of those who insult you fall*
> *on me."*

> *Psalm 69:9*

Many Pastors and their families do not have the same freedom that many church members have to recover completely after childbirth or a surgery. In my case during the birth of my children I was not able to take time to recover completely. With only thirty days after my son James' birth, I was already accompanying my husband to church meetings, leading the worship group, and ministering at services.

To the outsiders, it seemed like nothing had changed, but only the Holy Spirit of God knew the sacrifice I was making to be able to be there. Tears of pain and suffering washed off not only my face but also my soul during those days.

The zeal for the work of God led us to sacrifice many of our family moments and the period of my recovery. We became fully involved in the growth of the work of God. Although my healing was not accomplished in the way I desired, miracles began to happen in the lives of those around me. Somehow my physical illness was allowed for the purpose of the glorification of His name.

Criticism

A Christian must be prepared for criticism. In my case, as if being diagnosed with Fibromyalgia, a condition that has no known medical cure was not enough, I would also have to face destructive criticism from those who in a very un-informed way, launched hurtful and offensive words towards me.

During this period, I've learned that while the human being has an incredible ability to dedicate their lives to others, to reinvent themselves, and to help others, we also have a devastating ability to fight against everything that does not fit the standards of our normalcy.

There were many times when I heard comments saying that my health condition was attributed to possible hidden sins or lack of forgiveness. In some occasions, people told me that they could not understand how I submitted myself to pray for others, to see them healed and not receive the cure myself. Those were very hurtful words and moments.

However, I knew that it was clearly the voice of the our enemy, the accuser of our souls, who tried and still tries to stop my ministry. But I know the One in whom I trust and His word says: "I am convinced that he is able to guard what I have entrusted to him for that day." (See 2 Timothy 1:12)

In response to adversity, God encourages and enables me to help others. Even though pain and mental tiredness harass me, as soon as I start ministering at a service or event, I feel the supernatural power of God invading me. I spend hours praying for people after events, I know that I couldn't do if it was only with my strength.

I see lives being transformed, situations resolved, people's bodies and souls being healed, and God undeniably revealing His presence and power. So I know that I am more than a conqueror I cannot stop repeating that my emotional healing happened so I could bring words of life and hope to those who seek their own healing.

Steps of faith

Another fundamental truth that my experiences with the Lord brought to light has been taking steps of faith. Let me try to illustrate with a personal testimony, in which I was not an instrument of healing to others but to myself. I was able to clearly see the power of God working in that particular situation.

One day I woke up, and my index finger was aching and swollen. At first, I didn't pay much attention to it, but as the day went on, the situation got worse. The index finger was so swollen that it could no longer bend it. As if that was not enough, the swelling passed to the second finger, and within a few days, it reached the third finger.

The pain became unbearable, and the swelling was such that the three fingers were almost thicker than my thumb. Slowly but surely I was losing the ability to use my right hand. My husband suggested that I should go to the doctor's as it looked like I had rheumatoid arthritis, and he was concerned about how quickly the swelling was spreading.

However, at that moment, I took a step of faith and decided that instead of going to the doctor's, I would speak to the doctor of doctors, Jesus Christ. (Note that I do not dismiss the need for medical attention. This situation was unique.) I took the anointed oil, anointed my fingers, and started walking inside the house, praying and rebuking that condition in the name of Jesus. I confess that if someone passing by on the street saw me praying that way, they would think I was crazy. But every step I took, I took it with determination and believing that I was already healed.

At the end of my prayer time, my fingers were still the same, swollen and sore, but inside me, I was convinced that I was healed. I stopped asking and started declaring that I was already cured. I spent the next three days just declaring my victory.

I constantly looked at my fingers and realized that the swelling had not reduce, but I had decided to believe, and no doubt would not be able to make me give up on my blessing. I knew that God was in control and that my healing had already been determined.

Finally, on the fourth day, I saw my fingers going back to normal and they were completely cured on the fifth day. I could move my fingers like nothing had ever happened for the glory of the Lord.

The most important lesson this episode taught me is that sometimes we are healed instantly, but other times, God tests our faith and allows healing to materialize after a few days or weeks. He is in control, and everything happens in the way and time that He determines.

We make a serious mistake when we want to teach God on healing rules or when and how He should perform miracles in our lives. Praise God, who does everything according to His own will. It is unimaginable the confusion it would create if miracles were done according to our will, or if God asked for our opinion on how to resolve disputes, who would be healed and how that was supposed to happen.

I praise the Lord that these decisions do not belong to us, and we should never want to take God's place, because He is perfect and almighty, and without Him, we couldn't do anything. We need to obey His directions and cultivate faith in him because only then will He act on our behalf. See what our Master teaches us:

"Jesus replied: Because you have so little faith. I tell you the truth, if you have faith as small as a mustard seed, you can say to this mountain, 'move from here to there' and it will move. Nothing will be impossible for you."

Mathew 17:20

CHAPTER 9

Miracles in the family

Our family is a gift from God to us, and a severe mistake anyone can make is to try to win the world and lose their own family. I have very clear in my mind that everything starts from inside our homes, and that our first ministry is to take care of those whom the Lord has entrusted to us:

> **"If anyone does not provide for his relatives, and especially for his immediate family, he has denied the faith and is worse than an unbeliever."**
>
> *1 Timothy 5:8*

To care for our families goes beyond economics, in terms of provision, or even affection, security, and other essential factors in maintaining a healthy family. Parents must dedicate themselves singularly to minister into their children's lives. What we do, speaks louder than what we say. We should lead our family by example.

It all starts at home

As I have mentioned a few times, my mother was a tremendous spiritual example to me; she was a woman of prayer, with a deep relationship with God, and I could see many being touched by God through her life of faith and devotion. That is what I try to pass on to my children, allowing them to see what God, by His mercy, has worked through me and motivate them to allow God to use them as miracle workers as well.

Whoever read my first book, Restoration – Leaving the Pain Behind, knows that my children are wonderful miracles of the Lord, and I don't allow them to forget that. In this chapter tough, I would like to focus on the miracles that we witness daily as a family. To better illustrate it, I will share with you a brief testimony about it.

Details

Here in the United States, it is very common to have bathtubs instead of the shower box in the bathroom of the houses, and our bathtub had been clogged for several weeks. My husband and my brother had already done what they could to solve that dilemma: they had previously used machines, products of various types, and my brother even removed the pipes, but nothing solved the situation.

How realistic is it for anyone and much more for a pastoral family to have to manually empty the water out of the bathtub every time someone uses it? We are very busy and are constantly attending activities in the church, running the visiting ministry and other tasks and in all honesty, emptying the bathtub for everyone every day was not part of our agenda, or at least it shouldn't be.

If we needed to arrive at church early for prayer or any meetings, we had to start getting ready at two in the afternoon. That was an unsolvable situation, and it was not for lack of interest, or lack of trying to resolve it. The plumber himself had already given up on the project, and we were worn out by it all.

But on a particular day, I've got tired of that situation. I concluded that the case of this bathtub was only going to be solved through prayer. I said to myself: Jesus has the power to reach out and break up the clog wherever it is! So, I called James, my youngest son, to help me, and together we prayed and ordered the end of that clogging issue with authority.

It didn't take long, and we heard a noise, the pipes started shaking, and the water started to drain instantly. James was astonished by the Lord's power and commented that God does hear prayers. I was delighted that my son witnessed that miracle, that response from God. The Lord hears the cry of a righteous person.

My children often ask me to pray for them, and we rejoice together in the presence of God. Andrew, my firstborn, always says that he asks God for a wife in the same way as my husband asked for me. He says that he wants his future wife to love God as much as I, his mother, love God. Nothing is more important to me than being an example for my children, because the first people Jesus called us to heal are those of our own family.

This is just one testimony of many in which we saw God at work as a family. And I cannot emphasize enough

      ELAINE DASILVA

that the most important thing is for you to be a channel of healing in your home, to be a person of prayer knowing that God is interested in manifesting His power through your life, especially among your family.

Edifying the home

So I invite you to use the next five minutes to pray for your family. It is our responsibility to present them in prayer before God. I like the slogan of the Deborah Project: "Parents on their knees, children on their feet". My personal motto is that my children need to be impacted by God before I can do God's work elsewhere.

I glorify God for my husband's life because together, we have first built our home. Then we have been able to embrace the ministry that God has given us, to be an instrument in the restoration of marriages. We have witnessed the miracle in the lives of several couples who no longer had any hope of reconciliation, whose marriages were completely destroyed, but were now restored by the Lord's grace.

Dear reader, if I could for a minute, take you back to my childhood, show you my heart at that point in history and allow you to live some of those moments with me, you would now celebrate my happiness and cure today. I literally live a NEW LIFE. A life that is cured of several traumas and abuses, a life of restored dreams, a true story re-written by God.

I am a living witness of the miracle of Jesus Christ in the lives of those who submit to Him. I am a very happy person and I feel privileged for being chosen to be in the ministry serving God and especially for being able to pastor the Ebenezer Baptist Church alongside my husband. We are happy to testify that they have also experienced the miracles of the Lord in their lives.

CHAPTER 10

Miracles in the church

Our church members are witnesses of the great miracles God has operated in our midst. Seeing the manifestation of God's power in our congregation is an enormous privilege and based on God's word it should be a constant as God promises great victories for His servants:

> *"Worship the Lord your God, and his blessing will be on your food and water. I will take away sickness from among you."*
>
> *Exodus 23:25*

Our church is our second family. As I mentioned previously, we need to live what we preach to have an impact on people's lives. Every time I am with church members, I am reminded by God that I was healed to spread healing to as many people as needed.

That means that miracles need to happen in the church as well; church members need to see salvation, deliverance, and restored lives, starting with their own. For this reason, I would like to share a testimony that had an impact in the whole church that we are privileged to pastor.

Touched since the womb

In 2012 I was at home praying in my office when I got a call from a young lady who congregates with us. She was pregnant and was crying a lot. Her anguish was so great that she could barely speak, and had to stop and catch her breath before telling me what was happening. Amid the tears, she finally shared with me that her doctor shared with her that the result of the ultrasound of her baby, showed the baby having Down syndrome.

We started to pray, and God gave me two messages to be passed on to her. First, He said that her baby was already completely healed. The second part of the message was for her husband, who, until that day, had a difficult personality, especially about her faith and being involved in church.

That man's heart was closed to the Gospel. What he did not know was that through the difficult situation they were facing, salvation would finally come into his life. After the prayer, I asked the young mother-to-be permission to go to her house and she allowed me to. I went to visit them that same evening at 7 o'clock.

Upon my arrival at their house, he was quite agitated. In anticipation to my arrival his wife had shared God's message about the baby's healing with him already which allowed him to have his mind more open. I was very direct and straight to the point and told him that God's time for his life had come.

Even though he was still agitated, he wanted to know if the baby was actually cured and would be born healthy. He wanted to test the conviction of my faith and make sure that God worked through my life. In his simple words and expressions of panic and concern, he told me that he would serve God from that moment on if the child was actually healed.

To his surprise, with God's authority and boldness from heaven, because I know in whom I believe, and knowing that the message had come directly from heaven's throne, I declared that he could safely surrender to God because the baby was healed. I also committed to go with her to the next ultrasound to witness in person to the great miracle that God performed.

Testifying the miracle

The following week I accompanied her to Boston Medical Center for her appointment. To the amazement of the ultrasound technician, she no longer saw what she had seen in the previous appointment. She was agitated and excused herself to see the obstetrician. We were put in a waiting room, and while we waited, I told the baby's mother to be calm because she would see God in action.

The doctor could not explain what was happening. She then shared that in the previous appointment, in addition to the Down syndrome she had noticed that the baby also had some defects caused by genetics. Now they were not finding those details in the images of that current ultrasound.

From the details the doctor shared with us, the previous test showed parts of the baby as a deformed mass and not as a complete child, and now the tests surprised them. The baby now had a little body perfectly developed and formed for the glory of God.

The obstetrician then recommended other tests to ensure that the child was healthy, one of the tests could present a serious risk to the child. The baby's mother knowing of God's deliverance and cure for the baby, opted not to have the test done.

A few months later, that child was born, and today he is a healthy, intelligent, creative, and handsome boy! Every time I see him, I always refer to him as my miracle, and the whole church learned of God's action and grew in faith and trust with this testimony.

The church needs to be a place of healing, where the signs are manifested and where people can learn in practice that we serve a God who is not limited, but is able to perform miracles and use us as channels of his blessings. All we have to do is to put our faith in action.

CHAPTER 11

The secret

Only God knows how honored I am to share with you these testimonies that I have lived, and to encourage you to believe that He has great miracles to perform in your life as well.

I am sure that this book is coming into the hands of people seeking for physical, mental, and even spiritual healing and God allowed you to have it, because He wants to heal you. I also know that this material will arrive in the hands of those who believe in the power of God and want to be used to heal others.

I can attest to everyone that there is a secret for miracles to happen, and that secret is called a life of prayer. It is common not to experience greater miracles because our faith is not being exercised or we do not spend enough time with God to understand His will, and to surrender completely to him.

Let's take a look at Abraham's life: a man of great faith and obedience. Imagine the situation in which he found himself in when facing God's difficult request, which was that Abraham would have to sacrifice his own son. I invite you to think of his anguish and the battle that was probably happening in his mind. We know that God would not let him sacrifice his son, but Abraham still did not know what deliverance was to come.

Still, that man maintained his faith and believed that God, the same God who had taken him out of the land of the Chaldeans and promised him, numerous descendants, was in complete control of his life. I confess that I almost lose my breath just thinking about Abraham's courage in doing that. These are moments in which we must deny ourselves and our will to please God. By doing that, all our efforts and sacrifices will be rewarded. See what the Word teaches us:

> *"The sacrifices of God are a broken spirit; a broken and contrite heart, o God, you will not despise."*
>
> *Psalm 51:17*

Our common excuse not to pray enough is that God knows us much better than we know ourselves, for He is our Creator. We know from the Scriptures that before we open our mouths, the Lord already knows what we are going to ask for. However, He does not tell us not to pray; on the contrary, He teaches us and encourages us to seek His presence, the GOD who can do and knows everything.

God is pleased when in prayer we tear our hearts out before Him and speak like a child who comes to his father, presenting Him with all his needs. He wants us to in detail describe everything we need before Him. For every good father seeks to do what's best for his children, and he will do all that is in his power to fulfill their needs.

If a human parent does that, are you able to imagine what the Lord Jesus is willing to do for us when we pour out ourselves before Him? Consider the love in God's eyes as He collects our prayers and the satisfaction of responding to our requests and meeting our needs.

God does not use favoritism when he answers our prayers, nor does he fail to comply with my request because there is a more urgent or a greater need ahead of mine. He loves us equally with agape love and has in His reservoir, blessings, and answers for all who seek His face. And whatever we ask according to His will, will be fulfilled even if it takes some time.

> *"And I will do whatever you ask in my name, so that the Son may bring glory to the Father. You may ask me for anything in my name, and I will do it."*
>
> *John 14:13-14*

Listening to God in dreams

The Bible reports on several passages in which God reveals His plans to His servants through dreams. And since He is an immutable God, even today, he continues to reveal Himself in the same way. It has not been different with me. Let me share with you an experience that shows that.

In Genesis 37, we read Joseph's fascinating story, in which God reveals his future through dreams. He suffered envy on the part of his brothers, who fervently desired his death, and that even his father was frightened about these dreams and said that he would not prostrate himself before his son.

However, despite the negative reactions, the dreams came true when he became the Prince of Egypt. That is how God does it when He reveals or promises something to us; it will certainly be fulfilled regardless of how long it takes or the difficulties faced during the preparation process.

It is not my intention to spread the idea that all dreams come from God. However, some dreams are revelations, and we can discern it by the way we feel when we wake up. When God reveals something through a dream, it will come to fruition, and He also compels us to seek Him in order to show us the deliverance He will give us.

In September 2019, I had a dream about a person who congregated with us. In the dream, she was crying, a cry of despair because of a dire situation she was facing and needed help. In the dream, I prayed for her, so immediately upon waking up in the morning, I prayed for her life.

After that, I continued my activities, and in that evening, me and other members of the church went to the church to decorate it in preparation for the launch of my first book the next day. One of the ladies was sick, and without delay, I prayed for her. I then saw the person I saw in my dream and asked to talk to her.

Until that moment, I didn't know exactly how to pray for her, but knowing that God knows all things and that He puts the right words in my mouth when I pray for people, I started to pray. Immediately after I began, God sent me the message to rebuke an illness and the spirit of death that was over that woman. While praying, I noticed that she was crying and at the same time she was taking possession of her victory in Jesus' name.

What God wanted to do did not stop there. On Sunday, in the morning meeting, during the worship period, Jesus led me to pray for the sick and continue rebuking all diseases. While I prayed, I asked people to put their hand on the site of their illness, and to take possession, by faith of their cure. We spent amazing moments in the presence of the Lord.

During the same week, the lady I had dreamed about, told me that she was healed. She shared with me that when I mentioned the dream and prayed for her, she courageously took possession of her healing. She said that she was experiencing a severe illness and that the only person who knew about its severity was her son, as she wanted to prepare him for her death.

She even showed him the sizable lump that was in her breast, and the tests had found a cancer that was already in final stages. The doctor made it clear that the prognosis was not good, so she advised her son to get ready for her departure.

To my delight and confirmation that God speaks in many ways, during the ministry on Sunday, she also laid her hand on the disease and believed it was time to be freed from that malady. When she got home, she immediately looked for the lump and it was gone. Her son was amazed and happy, and she also shared her testimony before the church, where everyone celebrated her cure with her.

When she returned to the doctor, none of the tests showed the lump anymore, and no matter how hard the doctor tried to find it, the disease was no longer there. That health professional tried to find an explanation, but he couldn't. The tumor than once was visible to the naked eye, now couldn't be found. The doctor had no choice but to accept that something divine had happened.

She got to know Jehovah-Rapha, the God who heals more closely. I would like to encourage you, dear reader, to also get to know Him. Stand firm in faith and believe that He can do anything and that He reveals Himself to us in many different ways, including through prophetic dreams. Open your heart to start experiencing these manifestations in your life. God's word says:

> *"And these signs will accompany those who believe: In my name they will drive out demons; they will speak in new tongues; they will pick up snakes with their hands; and when they drink deadly poison, it will not hurt them at all; they will place their hands on sick people, and they will get well."*
>
> *Mark 16:17-18*

CHAPTER 12

Exercising Faith

> *"Is anyone of you sick? He should call the elders of the church to pray over him and anoint him with oil in the name of the Lord. And the prayer offered in faith will make the sick person well; the Lord will raise him up. If he has sinned, he will be forgiven."*
>
> *James 5:14-15*

Earlier, we talked about the importance of divine signs for the edification of our church, and reading this verse, I realize that the members of our congregation know that they can always count on us to pray for them. It is great to know that they feel comfortable to share their loads with us and together we present those situations before God.

Just over a month after the testimony in which God healed our friend from the lump in the breast, another lady approached me after the service to ask for prayer. She told me she had a sore throat, and hoarseness that now had stolen her voice. She had to make a great effort for her voice to come out, and was quite unwell. We prayed, and she went to her appointment.

After some tests, the doctor explained that she had a lump in her throat and would need surgery. The diagnosis showed a malignant tumor. What a difficult time that was. She felt her heart collapse inside her and was invaded by panic and even fear of dying.

She could not stop thinking about her husband and her teenage daughter, who, in turn, were also disoriented, fearing to lose her, as they could not bear the thought of a life without her.

Despite that situation, she shared the results with me and asked me to pray for her. I immediately took the oil, anointed her, and we cried out to God, as I rebuked that lump in Jesus' name. When praying, God instructed me to tell her to calm her heart and rest in Him because the doctors would not find anything in the next tests. From that day on, she was completely healed.

As she had not yet experienced such a miracle until that day, her heart remained shaken, and her mind struggled with the uncertainty of this divine operation. But as we read in Hebrews 11:1, "Now faith is being sure of what we hope for and certain of what we do not see." This way, that sister would need to position herself as one who saw the supernatural.

Overcoming unbelief

In our journey, we will face situations in which we will need to exercise our faith, to activate it. Faith is like a muscle that needs constant stimulation, or it becomes stunted, inoperative. As we give it the necessary attention and work towards strengthening it, it becomes more resilient and stronger, and increases our ability to face problems with the right attitude.

What happened to her is very common. Sometimes we love God above all things, but depending on the situation we are facing, as humans, we are attacked, and our minds become our greatest adversary. With the uncertainty of her future, she had planned to return to Brazil as she thought that it would be easier on her family in the event of her passing.

Once her new appointment had been scheduled, she went to church, and met my husband, Pastor Agnaldo. Once again, she opened her heart and cried for help. She also mentioned that I had already prayed for her. She went as far as mentioning that, directed by God, I told her that she could rest because the work of God in her life had already been done. With this information, my husband looked at her and said: "So, listen to her and rest. If God directed Pastor Elaine to tell you that, just trust her!"

After a few days, the so frightening time to return to the doctors had come. Needless to say, to her surprise, everything happened the way the Lord had said. His promise had not changed; He always keeps His promises.

The doctor could not find anything and said that something strange had happened in her throat. To his amazement, on the spot where the tumor once resided, there was only a scar left. Praise the Lord! God performed the surgery and left that scar there so everyone could believe that He, the doctor of doctors, and the Lord of Lords had operated on her.

She later on, came to the Sunday service with her husband and her daughter to give her testimony before the congregation. Her and her family wept with joy, satisfaction, and contentment for the miracle received. Many of the other church members were also crying, and everyone delighted with that remarkable and beautiful moment. Praise God!

> *"For I know the plans I have for you, declares the Lord, plans to prosper you and not to harm you, plans to give you hope and a future. Then you will call upon me and come and pray to me, and I will listen to you. You will seek me and find me when you seek me with all your heart."*

> *Jeremiah 29:11-13*

God's command and His intentions about us are clear. He did not create us to drift away, but He left us His Word for our comfort and to be a compass for our living. Through His word, we are encouraged to seek healing in all aspects of our lives.

> *"Heal me, o Lord, and I will be healed; save me and I will be saved, for you are the one I praise."*

> *Jeremiah 17:14*

God favors us and wants to bless us. We just need to get out of our comfort zone and search for Him. We need to breakthrough in faith. We need to seek more of His presence, develop an intimate and profound communion with the Holy Spirit, and an intense relationship with Jesus. The heart of God is always ready to answer us:

"If you then, though you are evil, know how to give good gifts to your children, how much more will your Father in heaven give the Holy Spirit to those who ask him?"

Luke 11:13

"Ask and it will be given to you; seek and you will find; knock and the door will be opened to you... your Father in heaven give good gifts to those who ask him!"

Mathew 7:7 / 11

God wants to act; He is just waiting for us to take the first step towards Him. To illustrate it better, let me share one more story of a physical and spiritual miracle that only happened because the person wanted more from God.

Renewed faith

On Fridays, we have a service dedicated to deliverance and healing in our church. On a particular day, a certain sister asked for prayer because her back was bothering her. She realized that her movements were not the same, which caused pain and discomfort. As I laid hands on her, I felt that God wanted to heal her physically and spiritually.

As I began to pray for her, the power of God was so intense in that place that she couldn't stand, and there on the church's floor, God renewed her. When she got up, she no longer felt any discomfort, and her back allowed for normal activities once again. The gratitude to God was immeasurable; for that day, her faith was strengthened, and her vigor restored.

That illness had prevented her from attending church meetings regularly, and discouragement had taken hold over her. Now, she was free to worship God in the temple once again. Upon arriving home, she shared the healing experience with her husband, who was also revived with that news, and together they now continue to seek the almighty.

Obedience equals miracles

Another fundamental aspect of the search for God is obedience. When we obey God, the miracle will happen in any area of our lives we need it to. The Bible teaches us that "to obey is better than sacrifice" (see 1 Samuel 15:22). But how many times do we deceive ourselves by fasting, obeying rituals, while disobeying God unashamedly when He asks us to do something that is not for our benefit?

I wish we could see the people around us with God's eyes for a few seconds, and love them with the love that He loves them, and dare to sacrifice ourselves for others who need us. Let's make a decision to obey Him more and we will experience the profound results of doing it.

I remember a service back in 2015. I was literally dragging myself; I didn't use a cane or a crutch because I didn't have them at home. I had dislocated my back, and the pain was greater than my strength. I had taken pain medication, gotten massages, used a cream common among athletes, and even another cream used on horses, which a lady from church had told me about.

I had done everything I could, yet with no positive results. Due to Fibromyalgia (note that I do not call this disease my own, it is affecting me, but it doesn't belong to me), conventional methods and remedies rarely work, as the body becomes resistant to pain medication. The muscles have a hard time recovering and any incident becomes more challenging to overcome.

But let's go back to the Sunday service. I was in the pulpit to minister the moment of worship and praises to the Lord and lead the church to worship God together with our worship team. As soon as I started ministering God spoke firmly in my ears in an impactful and clear way saying: "Stop the songs and start praying for My healing over the sick."

Without any delay, I stopped the worship and shared with the church what God had told me. I obeyed God's command, and His presence was poured out in that place in such way that reminded me of how His presence invaded the tabernacle in the Old Testament:

> *"Then the cloud covered the Tent of Meeting, and the glory of the Lord filled the tabernacle."*
>
> *Exodus 40:34*

Unexpectedly God touched my back and put it back in place. What a pleasant surprise the Lord Jesus gave me! While I obeyed His command to pray for others, He did for me what I needed most. After that day, my back didn't dislocate anymore.

Jehovah-Rapha, the God who heals, healed me and wants to heal you too. Just believe, persevere and obey Him, and you will be surprised with the wonders He will operate in you and throughout your life.

> *"But the man who looks intently into the perfect law that gives freedom, and continues to do this, not forgetting what he has heard, but doing it – he will be blessed in what he does."*
>
> *James 1:25*

     ELAINE DASILVA

CHAPTER 13

Attitudes that heal

By reading this book to this point, you already know that God wants to heal you, and above all, to make you a healing instrument for other people. After all, the true meaning of the Gospel is that we can serve others as our Master did. That is why I invite you to reflect on how impactful our participation can be in healing people.

We know that there are things that are not up to us to resolve. Topics that go beyond our human capacity. With that being said, there are behaviors and a certain posture that we can take to be used by God as a healer, and that is the topic I would like to reflect with you on this chapter. In the next several paragraphs I will share with you behaviors that make us vessels of blessing and tools of transformation in the lives of others:

 ELAINE DASILVA

1 – PROPHESIZE BLESSING WORDS

We know that what flows from our lips has the power to bring life or death, so our mouths need to be a channel of blessing, healing, life, and peace. God's Word is filled with words that we can prophesize over our lives and the lives of those around us.

As bad as someone's situation may be, if we declare the word of God over the person with firm faith, we can trust that God will resolve the situation. We also need to rebuke the Devil with authority in the name of Jesus and celebrate the victory. I like a verse in Isaiah that I have used it many times in my prayers:

> *"From the west, men will fear the name of the Lord, and from the rising of the sun, they will revere his glory. For he will come like a pent-up flood that the breath of the Lord drives along."*

> *Isaiah 59:19*

Let us seek victory in God, and if the devil rises against us, we have no reason to fear because the Holy Spirit will raise the flag of victory against him.

2 – PRAY FOR THE PERSON

> *"Pray for each other so that you may be healed. The prayer of a righteous man is powerful and effective."*

> *James 5:16*

Prayer will always be one of the main pieces in the victory puzzle. There is no way to be victorious, to bless others, and to fight in the spiritual realm if we do not pray.

If we ask, God will give us the wisdom on how to pray for miracles with faith and believing in His power.

> *"Call to me and I will answer you and tell you great and unsearchable things you do not know."*
>
> *Jeremiah 33:3*

We must be careful not to pray against God's will. If someone is sick and we start asking God to shorten their suffering by anticipating their death, while their prayer request was for healing, we will be bringing sadness and lack of faith to the sick person. I have met people who, because of their own interests, prayed for someone's death instead of prophesying life. Our prayer needs to be like Paul's prayer for the Philippians:

> *"And this is my prayer: that your love may abound more and more in knowledge and depth of insight, so that you may be able to discern what is best and may be pure and blameless until the day of Christ, filled with the fruit of righteousness that comes through Jesus Christ — to the glory and praise of God."*
>
> *Philippians 1:9-11*

Everything we do needs to be done in love; we need to put ourselves in the shoes of the person for whom we are praying, interceding, or fasting. This process will not be easy, but the satisfaction of witnessing people being transformed and healed is priceless.

There is such satisfaction in knowing that God, the Almighty, has enabled you to overcome obstacles and many uprisings from hell so that someone, who was hurt, could be transformed. All honor and glory be given to Him, our sovereign God.

> *"For from him and through him and to him are all things. To him be the glory forever! Amen."*

> *Romans 11:36*

We need to have a level of intimacy with God through prayer so that He can use us for the Glory of His name. Let us be men and women of prayer. The world we live in needs prayer intercessors, people who pay the price in prayer so miracles can happen.

> *"Do not be anxious about anything, but in everything, by prayer and petition, with thanksgiving, present your requests to God. And the peace of God, which transcends all understanding, will guard your hearts and your minds in Christ Jesus."*

> *Philippians 4:6-7*

Once again, God instructs us to pray without ceasing as the Word of God relates "pray continually" (see 1 Thessalonians 5:17). Pray with faith and lay before Him all the causes we are fighting for, and with that He, the good God will bring peace, tranquility, and answers to our requests.

3 – SHARE A BIBLE VERSE

The Bible will always be the right and precise source of words we should use. This age of technology has placed in our hands different opportunities for us to spread the Word of God. We have access to WhatsApp, E-mail, Facebook, Instagram, Twitter, and many other channels that I am unacquainted with yet.

However, unfortunately, social media is commonly used to share information that does not bring any secular nor spiritual enlightenment. As Christians, we have an opportunity, to revolutionize these channels and bring healing, deliverance, and salvation of souls for the kingdom of God.

Make a commitment before God to send people around you Bible verses through the media channels you have available to you. Feel free to also make phone calls to bless those in need of healing. Below are some examples of bible verses we can use:

> *"Surely he took up our infirmities and carried our sorrows, yet we considered him stricken by God, smitten by him, and afflicted. But he was pierced for our transgressions, he was crushed for our iniquities; the punishment that brought us peace was upon him, and by his wounds we are healed."*
>
> *Isaiah 53:4-5*

> *"Dear friend, I pray that you may enjoy good health and that all may go well with you, even as your soul is getting along well."*
>
> *3 John 1:2*

> *"My son, pay attention to what I say; listen closely to my words. Do not let them out of your sight, keep them within your heart; for they are life to those who find them and health to a man's whole body."*
>
> *Proverbs 4:20-22*

Make it a habit to bless others with the Word of God. Don't just do it once in a while, but make a note and add it to your schedule or calendar, and don't lose focus to spread God's Word with those who need it.

4 – BE A FRIEND

Friendship is something wonderful that cannot be found just anywhere or around the corner. A friendship is built through and with love. True friends are with us at all times and through any circumstance, without judgment.

Finding a true friend is a rarity in the world we live in today; it is like finding a pearl of great value. As servants of God, we must be sincere, and when we decide to offer our friendship to someone, we must act loyally and imitate Christ's behavior.

> *"A man of many companions may come to ruin, but there is a friend who sticks closer than a brother."*
>
> *Proverbs 18:24*

> *"A friend loves at all times, and a brother is born for adversity."*
>
> *Proverbs 17:17*

How can we guarantee that our friends will never betray us? In fact, we cannot do that. But regardless of this factor, our healing and complete restoration must continue being the center of our focus. Always remember that our friend Jesus, the friend of friends, will never fail and will never give up on us.

I understand that many people never had a true friend to share their pain, their moments of sadness and weaknesses with. The first move is to invite Jesus to be our best friend and with His guidance invite others to be part of our lives. Allow Jesus to embrace you today. Feel His love for you, and open your heart, letting Him live in you from now on.

> *"Greater love has no one than this, that he lay down his life for his friends. You are my friend if you do what I command. I no longer call you servants, because a servant does not know his master's business. Instead, I have called you friends, for everything that I learned from my Father I have made known to you."*
>
> *John 15:13-15*

I never get tired of reading and rereading these verses, because I see the love of God for all of us clearly shown in them. My desire is for these verses to be an invitation to us to become trustworthy friends and make those around us feel as loved by the Lord as we already feel.

5 – MAKE A VISIT

Visiting people with no personal interest, just to help them, has become a rarity. Our daily rush has been our excuse and has prevented us from taking a few minutes to bless others.

We no longer hear of many people cooking a meal for someone who is sick, or visiting someone who doesn't move easily, let alone visiting people with emotional illness. If we could understand the value of a visit and especially when people can testify of our pure intention to help them, we would be more active in this area.

I remember a man who was at home praying, and God sent him to the supermarket. Upon his arrival, God told him to hug the young man that was passing by him, and to tell him that Jesus loved him. He obeyed the voice of God regardless of his fear of what people could think of him.

Immediately the young man started to cry and shared that his life had been a valley of suffering, he felt worthless, and that it was the first time he heard and felt that someone actually loved him. As the conversation continued, he confessed to that man his suicide plan.

The young man had planned to get home and, with a gun that was already prepared, shoot himself in the ear. He was convinced that suicide was the only way out. That gentleman now offered him the opportunity to surrender to Christ. He invited him to allow Christ be the center of his existence, and receive Him as Lord and savior of his life, to which the young man promptly accepted.

Together they made the confession prayer, and from that moment on, God began the healing process in that young man's life. By the obedience of that servant of God, Jesus saved and forgave the young man's sins and delivered him not only from physical but also from eternal death.

> *"That if you confess with your mouth, "Jesus is Lord," and believe in your heart that God raised him from the dead, you will be saved."*
>
> ***Romans 10:9***

Who knew a hug could be so important? We live in a society thirsty for love and encouragement. People live in despair going from home to work, work to home, or college, and find no rest for their souls, and many of them are just desperate to receive a hug.

If you feel the direction of God to make visits, start to sanctify yourself now, so that when God indicates where to go, you are prepared and can be a blessing to those visited by you. We need to be vigilant not to act out of our emotions or need to show others that we are obeying God.

> *"But when you give to the needy, do not let your left hand know what your right hand is doing."*
>
> *Mathew 6:3*

Let us not lose focus when doing God's work. We must never seek our own glory. Our reward is not here, but in heaven. We must also strive to be people who spread hope and not despair.

I cannot deny that sometimes God has directed me to deliver difficult to address messages. In those instances God also gives me the wisdom and the necessary insight on when and how to deliver what God is commanding me to say. I would like to emphasize that regardless of whether I am delivering a positive or difficult to hear message, I seek confirmation from God before saying anything.

I emphasize this topic because not every feeling we have come from God and depending on the subject, we need to pray and get God's confirmation to be sure that the message delivered is helping the recipients to achieve their healing.

I still remember when visiting this lady, a friend of many years, who was ill. When we arrived at her house we met several people there, as everyone loved her and wanted to be there for her. In an act of faith and unity, we held hands and prayed for divine intervention, because Jehovah-Rapha, the God who heals, was the only one who could heal her. We could feel the power of God in that place, and after that prayer, her husband and daughters were smiling certain of her cure.

However, to our surprise, one person that was there deliberately began to tell her daughters, that she would soon die and advised them to prepare for it. In a matter of minutes, the climate of peace and hope became a spiritual battleground with deep sadness accompanied by fear and lack of faith.

Immediately my husband and I warned everyone that God is the God of the impossible and that He was in control of that situation. I thank God that we were there while that scenario was undergoing because we were able to act quickly under the guidance of the Holy Spirit, and once again bring a word of hope to everyone.

For the glory of God, the sick lady was completely healed. Many years have passed since that episode and to this day she continues to stand firm and strong in her faith, serving Jesus with joy and gratitude, always praising God for His mercy in her life.

Therefore, I insist that we take all possible measures to be a channel of kindness, love, and faith, and not of despair. Words can be used devastate and destroy or build and bless. When visiting someone, we should fill the environment with praises, read the Bible and pray with the family or the person we are meeting with. If we pray with faith, the Lord will certainly respond to our requests.

> *"This is the confidence we have in approaching God: that if we ask anything according to his will, he hears us."*
>
> *1 John 5:14*

Let us present ourselves as examples of life to the wounded, acting in such a way that our neighbor feels helped and blessed by us. Also, share material blessings with others, such as clothes and shoes in good condition. A Bible to those who do not have one, a plate of food, or whatever is within your reach. My husband and I have lived by faith, sharing even the last we have, and God has rewarded us and poured out blessings beyond measure.

> *"If anyone has material possessions and sees his brother in need but has no pity on him, how can the love of God be in him?*
>
> *1 John 3:17*

Investing our time to bring joy to others, gives us more satisfaction than what those in the receiving end of our display of affection and compassion are getting. For as the Word of God teaches us: "It's more blessed to give than to receive" (see Acts 20:35).

6 – BE UNDERSTANDING

Another story that touches and inspires me greatly is the story of Hellen Keller. Helen Keller was only 19 months old when she lost her sight and hearing as a result of an illness that had affected her. This reality in Helen Keller's life left her depressed, aggressive, and without hope for a promising future until she met a teacher called Ann Sullivan.

This instructor understood her and helped her overcome the barriers created by her disabilities. Ann Sullivan understood the difficulties associated with blindness as she was almost blind herself. She also played a role in helping Helen Keller in her emotional healing process.

Ann Sullivan developed a teaching method using Helen's hands. She helped her to understand that regardless of her situation, it was possible to learn new things and improve herself. She provided Helen with hope and with the desire and the certainty that she could learn to read, write, and spell in Braille.

With the help of her mentor, Helen learned that her physical disability could be a difficult barrier to face, but it would not be the end of the road. The works "Empathy – Key to Kindness and Compassion" and "Summary of The Story of My Life: Helen Keller's Autobiography" report that Mrs. Sullivan certainly understood the emotional pain that Helen felt, as she was the first deaf and blind person to graduate in the area of Philosophy at a highly respected institute. Throughout her life, she defended social rights, especially those aimed towards people with disabilities.

Inspired by Ann Sullivan, Helen overcame obstacles and lived her life helping people who had similar disabilities as hers. All of that was possible, because one day, someone understood what she was going through.

> *"So long as you can sweeten another's pain, life is not in vain."*
>
> *Helen Keller*

When we are understanding and determine in our hearts to be participants in the creation of solutions and not problems, we can be a source of transformation in the lives of those who are hurting. Helen Keller's story could have been different, had it not been for the kindness of a teacher who believed Helen was capable of many things.

Physical and emotional problems can cause anxiety, depression, and even a change in temperament, and all of that with the person not realizing they are having these problems. People who have now recovered and are healed can testify that they did not understand why they were alone and shunned.

As victims of hurt people do not realize that their behavior alienates others, and in return, those close to them do not understand how to demonstrate kindness and compassion during this process of pain and suffering. This suffering affects their physical, emotional, spiritual, and intellectual lives.

Be the answer to someone's prayer, an agent of healing and transformation. We all have needs and problems, but the best we can do for ourselves is not to orbit around our own needs and reach out to others, demonstrating that way, the love of the God we profess to serve.

Attitudes that hurt

We covered in the earlier chapter some attitudes that can help in the healing process of people. Now I dedicate this chapter to tell you about what we should not do if we are committed to assist someone who needs healing. These are attitudes that I share based on my personal, pastoral, and psychological experiences, and I ask the Lord to make it enlightening to all who wish to be used by God.

1 – JUDGING

No matter how similar my situation is to yours, we will never have the same reaction or the same results. While for someone, a migraine that persists for months can be a normal fact of life, to another, it can be the last straw in a devastating situation.

I say this because when we put ourselves in the position of judges and jump to conclusions about someone's physical, spiritual, or emotional illness, we may be aggravating that person's condition. For example: if the problem was physical, our lack of understanding and support could create an emotional wound which in turn worsens the physical situation twice as much. So, what is the benefit that we bring to this situation when we add our judgment to it? What reward will we receive for aggravating someone's sadness?

According to the Priberam dictionary (a Portuguese language dictionary), judging is: "proceed to examine the cause of; decide (as a judge, arbitrator, etc.); sentence; form a judgment about; imagine; belief; suppose; take into account; pronounce a sentence; form a concept. Be a judge of yourself; evaluate yourself; believe yourself."

However, we cannot forget that God is our judge and Lord, and we cannot and should not take God's place to judge or criticize anyone. All of our works will be judged, and everything we do is connected not only with the principle of sowing but also with the fact that acting with love and kindness towards others is our obligation.

I like an expression my husband uses: "brothers, in His steps, what would Jesus do?" This phrase used by him is a title of a book and an evangelical movie too. As Christians, or even as just human beings, we need to be more like Jesus and act like Him more often.

There are countless situations in which Jesus was right, yet He decided not to judge, but reach out and help those who needed His help. Do you remember the woman caught in adultery? Or the blind that was healed by Jesus? And the oppressed people He freed?

Jesus healed and still heals today. We were also healed by Him spiritually, emotionally and physically, to be able to heal other people. Reflect with me in these biblical passages:

"You, then, why you judge your brother? Or why do you look down on your brother? For we will all stand before God's judgment seat."

Romans 14:10

"Do not judge, or you too will be judged. For in the same way you judge others, you will be judged, and with the measure you use, it will be measured to you. Why do you look at the speck of sawdust in your brother's eye and pay no attention to the plank in your own eye? How can you say to your brother, 'Let me take the speck out of your eye', when all the time there is a plank in your own eye? You hypocrite, first take the plank out of your own eye, and then you will see clearly to remove the speck of your brother's eye."

Mathew 7:1-5

"Do not judge, and you will not be judged. Do not condemn, and you will not be condemned. Forgive, and will be forgiven. Give, and it will be given to you. A good measure, pressed down, shaken together and running over, will be poured into your lap. For with the measure you use, it will be measured to you."

Luke 6:37-38

 ELAINE DASILVA

Today we have the opportunity to make an intelligent and conscious decision to avoid being instruments of judgment, and become instruments of healing. The Bible teaches us in Romans 12.2, not to conform with this world but to be transformed by the renewing of our minds. Then we will be able to experience God's will that is good and perfect. When we decide not to judge others, we and our families are blessed by God in ways we cannot imagine.

2 – SPEAKING ILL OF OTHERS

> *"If anyone says, 'I love God', yet hates his brother, he is a liar. For anyone who does not love his brother, who he has seen, cannot love God, whom he has not seen."*

> *1 John 4:20*

Look at the responsibility we have, since the Word of God teaches us to love our neighbors and speak well of people. Jesus being perfect, chooses to see the best in all of us, even though our flaws are not invisible to Him, He chooses to give greater importance to the good qualities that He has placed in us.

Let's meditate in this for a second: if Jesus saves and s restores the life of a criminal or serial-killer, and shows love and compassion for them, why do we sometimes want to take God's place and allow our human tendency to take over? When we speak ill of people, we open a door to the devil and attract a curse for our lives.

There is nothing more devastating than the deceitful spirit of a human being. There are people that in our presence will praise us, and even offer us their friendship, but once removed from our presence words of betrayal and destruction are part of their vocabulary. This attitude not only displeases God but brings spiritual and even physical destruction to those who choose this practice. Let us meditate on what James says:

> **"With the tongue we praise our Lord and Father, and with it we curse men, who have been made in God's likeness. Out of the same mouth come praise and cursing. My brothers, this should not be."**
>
> *James 3:9-10*

We cannot prevent people from approaching us to share information that they shouldn't be sharing. However, with kindness and Christian love, we can invite the person to pray for the individual who is not present, and let God take over the situation and bring the much needed solution.

Pleasing and obeying God is more important than pleasing people who maliciously try to include us in situations that do not contribute to anyone's wellbeing. Serving God and pleasing Him in any circumstances many times requires sacrifices and making difficult decisions. Do not be afraid of standing up and eliminating unnecessary conversations from our life.

Know that many individuals who need healing, have a lot of emotional needs and try to draw attention to themselves, even if for that they need to damage other people's image. Do not be part of this destructive team! We should not be an accomplice of destructive behavior that may bring destruction to those around us, independently if they are our neighbors, pastors, friends, etc.

The leadership of our churches have been called by God to the ministry and despite their flaws and downfalls they are to be respected and honored. Pastors, deacons, elders, and church workers in general, carry a very heavy spiritual responsibility and are under great scrutiny. Let us pray more for each one of them, and present them before God, with true love. Praying for them is a much more useful time of our time than making unnecessary comments. See what the Bible teaches us:

> *"Brothers, do not slander one another. Anyone who speaks against his brother or judges him speaks against the law and judges it. When you judge the law, you are not keeping it, but sitting in judgment on it. There is only one Lawgiver and Judge, the one who is able to save and destroy. But you — who are you to judge your neighbor?"*
>
> *James 4:11-12*

> *"Do not pay attention to every word people say, or you may hear your servant cursing you."*
>
> *Ecclesiastes 7:21*

If we say we love God, we must commit daily to obey Him, and not make room for evil influence. Lies and fabricated words against others can destroy lives. Bellow, we have added an analogy that can help us understand the danger of spreading false information and defamation words towards others:

"Imagine yourself, on a windy day, on the top floor of the tallest building you have ever seen. Now, open a bag full of feathers and throw them out the window. Is the task done?

Okay. Now, go downstairs, get out of the building, and collect every feather you tossed out from the top of the building. Are you telling me that this task is impossible? Yes, it is. And so are the untruthful, mean, spiteful, and inappropriate words we say about other people. They can never be collected back. Even if we go to great lengths to reach out as many people as possible, not everyone affected by our malice will know the truth. For just as the wind carried those feathers to unimaginable distances, so the words we say about others, whether good or bad, will reach inexplicable levels."

We are called to be a channel of life and healing. When we sow what is good, we can partake on the best of this land. Jesus has placed at our disposal the best seeds. So, let us not be contaminated with seeds of inferior value that the devil puts in front of us.

3 – ADVISING WITHOUT KNOWLEDGE

In many cases, the damage caused by wrong advice is more harmful than physical wounds. In my ministry, I have assisted people who felt lost and destroyed because of information they received based on human convictions.

As we mentioned in previous paragraphs, even if the situation that two people are facing are similar, the results or outcomes are usually not. Therefore, counseling without the necessary knowledge can become destructive and invalidates the purpose of the advice.

Another aggravating factor is that we know the Word of God. If the advice offered does not represent the biblical instructions, it is better to remain silent. The Bible places a heavy responsibility on those who cause others to stumble. Any counseling that goes against God's word is not an option.

A clear example is couples counseling. People who are experiencing crises in their marriage, where both are hurt and in need of healing, can become targets of selfish and non-biblical advice. In many cases, one of the spouses, or both, feel confident with the so called friend/counselor and share their difficulties, opening their hearts sharing the most intimate and private details. The down fall is that in most cases, because these counselors are not equipped with the Word of God and a sense of responsibility for the family as God's project, they may advise the couple in a detrimental way and cause even more wounds.

In the Word of God, we find hope, advice on how to behave as a spouse. The Bible also delineates our responsibilities as a husband or wife, and above all, how and when we should seek His presence. God's timing on answering our requests may not be what we wish for, however, waiting for Him and His answers is never a mistake.

When we wait for God's response, He doesn't only work on our immediate request, but due to His knowledge of who we are and what is happening, He will also uncover, address and resolve the root cause of the problem. We should not allow fear to prevent us from continuing fighting. We have to persevere, trust in Him and His time for our victory, submitting to His will at all times, because only He knows what is best for each one of us.

Many of us were victims of destructive counseling and because of that, now we carry wounds. However, today is a new day, a new opportunity, a new beginning to all who seek wisdom. So embrace the cause of Christ and the direction of a God who does not fail.

Pray and ask for God's guidance and look for someone qualified to help you. When we do our part, the Holy Spirit does His. By deciding to help ourselves, we may be taking the first step to allow God to use us to heal and transform the wounds of others around us.

> *"The fear of the Lord is the beginning of wisdom, and knowledge of the Holy One is understanding."*
>
> *Proverbs 9:10*

> *"For the Lord gives wisdom, and from his mouth come knowledge and understanding."*

Proverbs 2:6

> *"Wisdom is a shelter as money is a shelter, but the advantage of knowledge is this: that wisdom preserves the life of its possessor."*
>
> *Ecclesiastes 7:12*

Seek wisdom from God, and He will be responsible for giving you all the necessary training and will use you for the honor and glory of His name.

4 – MINIMIZING THE SUFFERING OF OTHERS

I've faced a lot of sadness which people comparing their suffering to mine. It was very disappointing when doctors, nurses and therapists compared what I was feeling with other patients, or described me as a hopeless cause. There were situations when they doubted the degree of pain that afflicted me. They would send me home empty handed and without any updated treatments or information.

In one of my flights, there was a flight attendant who, when I asked for her help with my carryon luggage, began yelling and stating that helping me with my suitcase was not part of her activities. Despite my efforts to explain my physical condition to her, she became irritated and hostile. If that wasn't enough she tried to prevent another passenger from helping me.

These insults made my physical pain even worse, not to mention the emotional pain, the feeling of helplessness, loneliness, and sadness. But God was always my confidant and helped me in these difficult times. Also, I always had the support of my husband, who very kind, suffering with me and enduring the insults that came from all directions. Many times I just did not share the insults with him to avoid seeing him hurting.

Can you remember the way you felt when someone said something like: I know what you are going through, I've been through the same situation! Do you remember the anguish that entered your heart because you could not even own your suffering?

Based on what you felt with the scenario above, I would like to advise you to have a different attitude when someone comes to you to share their suffering. You may say something like: "I cannot imagine what you are going through, but I would like to be able to help you and be a blessing in your life. I want to be able to help you carry this load!" these words will open doors to heal the pain and wounds of those who approach you and to honor and glorify the name of the Lord Jesus Christ. Think about it:

> **"Wise men store up knowledge, but the mouth of a fool invites ruin."**
>
> **Proverbs 10:14**

An example of how we humans tend to minimize the pain of others was when my youngest son, at the age of three, needed a corrective surgery on his left eye, to prevent vision loss. He had been wearing glasses since he was three months old, which had a huge impact on us. Can you imagine your baby wearing glasses?

Over time we've got used to the idea, and we even thought it was cute because the glasses were so tiny. In one of my next books, I will give more details of the miracle cures in James' life and his vision. But going back to the days before his surgery: A friend of ours felt a lot of compassion for us and James' situation, and with the best of intentions shared her concerns and care for us with another person.

The other lady, without any delay or details of the ordeal we were facing, minimized the problem by saying that eye operations are simple. But for a parent, there is no such thing as a simple operation, as a general anesthesia for a child with poor health will never be simple.

God is always in control, and we believe it. However, we are only human, and seeing our little son having to undergo a medical procedure like that, which took several hours to reconstruct the base of the muscles in his eye, brought us anguish and suffering.

I praise God that He, once again, was our comfort at that moment. Jesus said that in the world we would be afflicted, but that we should be brave, because He overcame the world, and with that, I was sure that everything would be fine.

> *"I have told you these things, so that in me you may have peace. In these world you will have trouble. But take heart! I have overcome the world."*
>
> *John 16:33*

We will never know what is coming our way, so it is essential to have compassion for one another. I would not be able to count how many times the people who despised me for my pain, or minimized my suffering or my family's anguish, were now coming to us asking for help. I thank God that during my healing process, He has taught me to love those who, with hate and fury has spoken and acted against our lives and ministry.

As servants of God, let us never engage in minimizing the pain of others, or comparing what they are going through with our situation. God allows us to go through difficult circumstances to use those situations to impact others. Be prepared; God wants to use YOU.

5 – AVOID DESTRUCTIVE WORDS

I am amazed at how God thought of all the details when He inspired the Bible writers to compose this Holly book that is our user's manual. All the necessary guidance for our human and Christian development are in it.

God, the sacred author, in His infinite wisdom, and knowing the particularities of each human being, left His instructions recorded for all of us. By making the reading of the Bible a daily routine, we will be ready to bless and be blessed.

As the verse above mentions, our words have power. We must think before we speak, hold on to our reasons and ask God to direct us to express what is right at the right time. We must learn to keep our words to ourselves and be prudent when using them, so that when we open our mouths, our words can have a more real and effective impact.

I particularly always ask God to purify my lips as He did with Isaiah. We are flawed and imperfect, but we have a perfect God who dwells in us. The responsibility of being vigilant with our words, so we do not prophesize destruction, is entirely ours.

We will never be able to justify ourselves before God for having used destructive language at the time of anger, or for thinking that we had the right to say so. Once again, I emphasize: our words have power, and it is our responsibility to use them wisely.

Let me share with you the story of a girl who came to us asking for help in prayer. Her soul was wounded, and her emotional health was devastated by the curse words constantly used by her mother towards her and her siblings' lives.

We are an emotionally damaged generation raising an even more unwell group of people. And this is one of the reasons why I decided to write this book because we need to take control of this situation and bring it to the presence of God for our healing to happen. With our cure we can influence our children and others around us to also seek God and the healing that He offers.

That young lady's mother, who most certainly was extremely wounded herself, in a moment of anger and lack of self-control, shouted the wish of a specific death to one of her children. To her desperation and the family's dismay, her words come to fruition in every detail, which left that young lady even more desperate and full of resentment. As she described the stories and this horrendous fact to us, our hearts felt her pain and sadness.

We then prayed together and she made the conscious decision to release forgiveness for her mother. , God healed her wounds, and today she is strong, continues to seek her emotional health and serves God faithfully.

We have before us the opportunity to become God's agents of healing in the lives of others, or agents of destruction and instruments that enhance human pain. God created us to be His representatives on earth. I would like to invite you to cast your old behaviors, attitudes and anything else that needs change before the cross today. Make the decision to be healed!

Conclusion

As I was writing and correcting his book, God spoke to me deeply and I learned from my own testimonies. I would like to wish you the same. May each page of this book bring you hope, comfort, and strength to your faith. Do not allow the wounds you carry at this moment to prevent you from being who God wants you to be. Christ is re-writing your history and has a purpose to be fulfilled in your life.

Close your ears to negativity, to words of defeat or even curse words that have been cast on your life. Make a decision to re-invest in your dreams. Our God is a God of new opportunities and has never given up on you. Rejection, mistreatment, abuse of all kinds, or any other event in your life won't change His love for you.

God does not look at us like humans do, but He looks at us with the love of a Creator who cherishes the work he has created, regardless of the wrong steps and thoughtless decisions we may have taken. We are His masterpiece, and He made us to live an abundant life.

As I mentioned before, if He does not remove the thorn from our flesh, He will give us the strength to overcome the obstacles caused by the thorn. With God at the center of our lives, wounds cannot control us, and our outlook in life will change completely.

Let us stop focusing on what is not essential and totally surrender before Christ. What is the use in conquering the world if for that we need to compromise our salvation? Having the body healed but the spirit sick? "What good is it for a man to gain the whole world, yet forfeit his soul?" (See Mark 8:36).

As a minister of the gospel, I declare that you will rise from the ashes, and you will be freed from the bonds that bind you right now. I proclaim that the devil's plan against your life, your marriage, and a better future for you are being destroyed this very moment. I declare that all hereditary curses, are being destroyed in the name of Jesus and that you are being healed and will continue your journey of healing and happines in the name of Jesus.

Dear reader, apply the principles presented in this book, and let God use you to heal others. You have been chosen to be a source of blessings. I also wish for your life testimony to travel around the world so that the name of Jesus can be proclaimed.

Never forget that you can do all things in Him, who strengthens you! You are now beginning a new chapter in your life, because the wounds you have suffered will turn your life into a path of victory, restoration, and healing. Never give up on this fight because you are not alone. Jesus is facing the storm with you, and His purpose will be entirely fulfilled and will be a channel of blessings for many others.

Get ready; your time has come!

Heal lives in the name of Jesus.

I conclude this book with a few brief words from those who received their healings, and whose stories were reported in this book:

"First of all, I thank God for my healing, and for giving Pastor Elaine Dasilva the gift of healing."

Fabricia Rodrigues

"I primarily thank God for sending me the Pastor to pray for me so that I could receive the healing of the lump in my throat. I also thank the whole church for their support."

Cristina Santa

"I thank God, and I thank Pastor Elaine for being with me at that difficult time. I am very grateful to you for having consoled us in the most difficult time of our lives."

Cleuza de Araujo

"Thank you, Pastor, for everything. Thank you, Pastor Elaine, for being a friendly and caring praying woman. God has used your life greatly."

Valdineia Viana

"For nothing is impossible with God. (Luke 1:37). With the strength of my faith, I managed to win this hard battle against the disease that consumed my body. Thank you, my God."

Paula Correa

"God allowed us to witness His power through the healing of my daughter Marina, who had suffered from lactose intolerance since she was three months old. While the Pastor prayed to God for her fever, she was healed in the name of Jesus from the fever and lactose intolerance. I am immensely grateful to God because He is good and acts on our needs."

Munique Macedo

With great affection, I also thank all of you who permitted me to publish your testimonies to glorify the name of our Lord Jesus. I love you.

If you, my dear reader friend, also have some testimony not reported here and would like to share it with me, please send an email to contato.elainedasilva@gmail.com.

Bibliography

TEAM: A Callery pear tree became known as the "Survivor Tree" after enduring the September 11, 2001 terror attacks at the World Trade Center. Available in: <https://www.911memorial.org/visit/memorial/survivor-tree> Accessed in April 2020.

TEAM: Empathy – The key to Kindness and Compassion. The Watchtower Announcing Jehovah's Kingdom – 2002. Available in: <https://wol.jw.org/pt/wol/d/r5/lp-t/2002285> Accessed in April 2020.

FRAZÃO, Dilva. Biografia de Helen Keller. Available in: https://www.ebiografia.com/helen_keller/>. Accessed in April 2020.

"Judge", in Dicionário Priberam da Língua Portuguesa [in line], 2008-2020, https://dicionario.priberam.org/julgar [consulted in 03-29-2020].

THE SACRED BIBLE. Portuguese/English. New International Edition. São Paulo: International Bible Society, 2017.